"Who wants to play hide-and-seek?"
Puddles gives a happy spray.

Puddles loves to play this game.
"You can hide and I will seek!"

Hide-and-Seek

ALL ABOUT LOCATION

Written by Kirsten Hall

Illustrated by Bev Luedecke

children's press®

A Division of Scholastic Inc.
New York Toronto London Auckland Sydney
Mexico City New Delhi Hong Kong
Danbury, Connecticut

About the Author

Kirsten Hall, formerly an early-childhood teacher,
is a children's book editor in New York City. She has been
writing books for children since she was thirteen years old
and now has over sixty titles in print.

About the Illustrator

Bev Luedecke enjoys life and nature in Colorado.
Her sparkling personality and artistic flair are reflected in her
creation of Beastieville, a world filled with lovable Beasties
that are sure to delight children of all ages.

Library of Congress Cataloging-in-Publication Data

Hall, Kirsten.
  Hide-and-seek : all about location / written by Kirsten Hall ; illustrated by Bev Luedecke.
    p. cm. — (Beastieville)
  Summary: When the Beasties play hide-and-seek, Puddles finds most of them in their favorite spots—but where
could Toggles be?
  ISBN 0-516-23649-0 (lib. bdg.)   0-516-25519-3 (pbk.)
  [1. Hide-and-seek—Fiction. 2. Stories in rhyme.] I. Luedecke, Bev, ill. II. Title.
  PZ8.3.H146Hid 2004
  [E]—dc22

                                                 2004000112

1 2 3 4 5 6 7 8 9 10 R 13 12 11 10 09 08 07 06 05 04

A NOTE TO PARENTS AND TEACHERS

Welcome to the world of the Beasties, where learning is FUN. In each of the charming stories in this series, the Beasties deal with character traits that every child can identify with. Each story reinforces appropriate concept skills for kindergartners and first graders, while simultaneously encouraging problem-solving skills. Following are just a few of the ways that you can help children get the most from this delightful series.

Stories to be read and enjoyed

Encourage children to read the stories aloud. The rhyming verses make them fun to read. Then ask them to think about alternate solutions to some of the problems that the Beasties have faced or to imagine alternative endings. Invite children to think about what they would have done if they were in the story and to recall similar things that have happened to them.

Activities reinforce the learning experience

The activities at the end of the books offer a way for children to put their new skills to work. They complement the story and are designed to help children develop specific skills and build confidence. Use these activities to reinforce skills. But don't stop there. Encourage children to find ways to build on these skills during the course of the day.

Learning opportunities are everywhere

Use this book as a starting point for talking about how we use reading skills or math or social studies concepts in everyday life. When we search for a phone number in the telephone book and scan names in alphabetical order or check a list, we are using reading skills. When we keep score at a baseball game or divide a class into even-numbered teams, we are using math.

The more you can help children see that the skills they are learning in school really do have a place in everyday life, the more they will think of learning as something that is part of their lives, not as a chore to be borne. Plus you will be sending the important message that learning is fun.

Madeline Boskey Olsen, Ph.D.
Developmental Psychologist

Bee-Bop

Puddles

Slider

Wilbur

Pip & Zip

Flippet

Pooky

Mr. Rigby

We're the Beasties

Smudge

Toggles

All the Beasties meet outside.
They do not know what to play.

Puddles covers up her eyes.
"I will make sure not to peek!"

Puddles tries to find her friends.
She thinks that she hears a noise.

It is Pooky. Puddles laughs.
Pooky is behind her toys!

Puddles starts to walk again.
She does not know where to look.

She looks in-between some rocks.
There is Bee-Bop with his book!

Off she goes to look some more.
She decides to look up high.

Flippet is above her head.
"I am lucky I can fly!"

Now she looks for Zip and Pip.
She wonders where they could be.

She looks over by the hill.
She looks high up in a tree.

"There are Zip and Pip!" she points.
They are hiding near the store.

Puddles opens her eyes wide.
"Were you hiding there before?"

Puddles looks for big Smudge now.
She thinks she knows where to go.

"I thought that you might be here!"
Big Smudge asks, "How did you know?"

Wilbur is not hard to find.
"I decided not to play."

He is right in front of her.
"Wilbur, you are in my way!"

Who is left for her to find?
Mr. Rigby! Where is he?

There he is inside the school!
"Good job, Puddles! You found me!"

Puddles looks for Slider now.
There he is below the slide!

Puddles laughs. "I see you there!
What a funny place to hide!"

There is only Toggles left.
Puddles asks, "What should I do?"

All her friends begin to laugh.
Bee-Bop says, "Look behind you!"

PLAYER COUNT

1. How many Beasties wanted
   to play hide-and-seek?

2. How many Beasties did NOT
   want to play the game?

3. How many Beasties are on the left side of
   the picture? How many are on the right?

LET'S TALK ABOUT IT

Finding all ten of her friends
was a lot of work.

1. Why do you think Puddles
   wanted to be the seeker?

2. What would have happened
   if she quit before finding everyone?

3. Which would you rather do,
   hide or seek?

SOUNDS LIKE...

"Creek" is a word that sounds
like "seek." Can you think of
any other words that
sound like "seek"?

WORD LIST

a	fly	in-between	over	thinks
above	for	inside	peek	this
again	found	is	Pip	thought
all	friend	it	place	to
am	friends	job	play	Toggles
and	front	know	points	toys
are	funny	knows	Pooky	tree
asks	game	laugh	Puddles	tries
be	gives	laughs	Rigby	up
Beasties	go	left	right	walk
Bee-Bop	goes	look	rocks	wants
Before	good	looks	says	way
begin	happy	loves	school	were
behind	hard	lucky	see	what
below	he	make	seek	where
big	head	me	she	who
book	hears	meet	should	wide
by	her	might	slide	Wilbur
can	here	more	Slider	will
could	hide	Mr.	Smudge	with
covers	hide-and-	my	some	wonders
decided	seek	noise	spray	you
decides	hiding	not	starts	Zip
did	high	now	store	
do	hill	of	sure	
does	his	off	that	
eyes	how	only	the	
find	I	opens	there	
Flippet	in	outside	they	